Anne Frank

Susanna Davidson

History consultant:
Eva Schloss, stepsister of Anne Frank

Reading consultant:
Alison Kelly, Roehampton University

You can find out more about Anne Frank, see film footage of her and read extracts from her diary by going to the Usborne Quicklinks Website at
www.usborne-quicklinks.com
and typing in the keywords *Anne Frank*.
Please note that Usborne Publishing cannot be responsible for the content of any website other than its own.

Designed by Natacha Goransky
Cover design by Russell Punter
Edited by Jane Chisholm
American editor: Carrie Armstrong
Digital manipulation by Mike Wheatley and John Russell
With thanks to Ruth King for her help with picture research

ACKNOWLEDGEMENTS

© **Corbis** p1 (Handout/Reuters), p5 (Reuters), pp5-6 (Royalty Free), p19 (Bettman), pp42-43, pp50-51 (Michael St. Maur Sheil), pp56-57 (Bettman); © **Getty Images** front cover (Anne Frank Fonds - Basel), p3 (Keystone Features), p6 (Anne Frank Fonds - Basel), pp8-9 (Anne Frank Fonds - Basel), p11 (Heinrich Hoffman/Timepix/Time Life Pictures), p12 (Anne Frank Fonds - Basel), p16 (Fox Photos), p22 (Anne Frank Fonds - Basel), p29 (Anne Frank Fonds - Basel), p40 (Anne Frank Fonds - Basel); © **Maria Austria Instituut** p39, p44; © **NIOD, Netherlands** pp18-19, pp20-21, p27, p36, pp48-49; © **Photoshot** p30; © **popperfoto.com** p17; © **Sebastián Castagna** p64; © **Topfoto.co.uk** back cover, pp30-31 (Ian Yeomans); © **USHMM** p7, pp14-15 (Bildarchiv Preussicher Kulturbesitz), p24 (top) (Harry Goldsmith Estate), pp46-47 (YIVO Institute for Jewish Research); © **Yad Vashem** (bottom) p24, p52, p54, pp60-61.

Contents

A photograph of children skating along a frozen canal near Amsterdam, where Anne grew up.

Chapter 1
Living free

A nne ran down the stairs and onto the
street as fast as she could, her skinny
legs going at full pelt. She was supposed to
be doing her homework, but it was so boring.
Margot, her perfect sister, might be happy
sticking her nose in a book all day, but
Anne wasn't.

She stopped when she reached the house
around the corner. Then she sang, breathlessly,
through the mailbox. Five notes up and five
notes down. It was her secret signal.

The next moment Lies Goslar, her best
friend, opened the door. Anne caught hold
of her hand and pulled her outside. "Come
on!" she said. "Let's go and play."

Their friend Sanne, and a crowd of other children, were already out on the sunny Amsterdam streets. Some were rolling hoops, others playing hopscotch or doing handstands against the wall. Anne was hopeless at handstands, but knew another way to get everyone's attention. "Watch this!" she cried, lifting her arm high in the air.

This photograph shows Margot and Anne in 1933. Margot is seven; Anne is four.

Here Anne is playing with her friend, Sanne, near the Frank's apartment in Amsterdam. Anne is the one on the right.

Anne waited until everyone was looking at her, then she swung her arm around as fast as she could. There was a loud CRACK! and her shoulder popped straight out of its socket. All the boys laughed and cheered.

Hearing the sound of laughter, Anne's mother, Edith, glanced out the window and caught sight of Anne on the street below.

"I bet that girl hasn't done her homework," she thought with a sigh. It was always such a struggle with Anne. Even though her daughter was only seven, Edith was certain she would be a social butterfly all her life.

Still, she was glad Anne had settled into Amsterdam life so easily. It was three years since the Franks had left Germany, but Edith still missed her home. And, as long as the Nazi Party ruled Germany, they couldn't go back. The Franks were Jewish and the Nazis hated Jews. Recently, the Nazis had fired Jews from their jobs, shut down Jewish shops and beaten up Jews on the street.

These Nazis are blocking the entrance to a Jewish-owned shop in Germany. The sign they are holding says, "Beware! Don't buy from Jews!" The photograph was taken in 1933, the year the Franks left Germany.

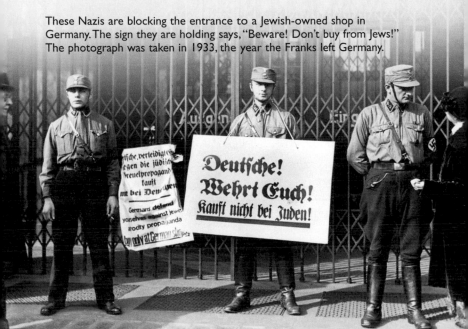

"We were right to leave when we did," thought Edith. "We couldn't have brought up our children in such a country."

That night, Anne's father, Otto, put Anne to bed as usual.

"Tell me a story!" Anne pleaded. "Can I have one about Good Paula and Naughty Paula? But this time tell me about Naughty Paula. She's more fun."

"Margot prefers Good Paula," Otto remarked.

"Well she would," Anne replied, huffily. It was hard having Margot as an older sister. She never got into trouble and was always neat and tidy.

Otto guessed what she was thinking. "You could be good, too, Anne. You just have to learn to control yourself."

"I'll try, Daddy, I promise," Anne said. "Anything to make you happy!"

Otto laughed. "You little flatterer," he said, kissing her on the head.

8

The next day at school, Anne tried harder than usual to concentrate. She loved school really – the big airy classroom, the bright red flowerpots on the windowsill... it was just so much more fun to talk to people than to listen to the lessons.

"Anne Frank, you are such a chatterbox," scolded her teacher.

"I can't help it, Mr. Keesing," Anne replied. "It's a female thing. My mother talks as much as I do and I inherited my talkativeness from her."

Everyone laughed, including the teacher.

A photograph of Anne's class taken in 1935.
Anne, circled here, is sitting at the back.

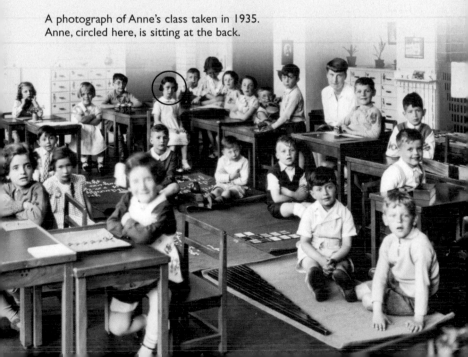

When Anne got back, Edith was bustling around the kitchen, preparing supper. "We have guests tonight," she said.

"Who's coming?" Anne asked eagerly.

"Miep, from Daddy's work, and her friend Jan."

"Hooray!" Anne cried. She loved it when people came around. As soon as the doorbell rang, Anne rushed to let them in. The next moment, she was peppering them with questions. "How are you Miep? How was your day? What's it like working for Daddy? Hello Jan!" Then Anne stopped and looked at them both, her brown eyes sparkling with interest. "Ooh! Are you Miep's boyfriend?" she asked.

"Quiet, Anne," interrupted Edith.

"Time for supper," added Otto, gently.

As soon as the meal was over, Anne and Margot were sent to bed.

"I expect they want to talk politics," said Margot.

"Or some sort of secret," Anne suggested. "Politics are boring."

"But things are getting worse," Margot explained. "It's all because of Hitler, the Nazi Party leader. He's making the Nazis more powerful than ever. They're building up a huge army."

Here you can see Adolf Hitler, directly facing the camera, at a Nazi Party rally in Germany. You can just make out the crowds of supporters in the background. The bent crosses on the flags are swastikas, the symbol of the Nazi Party.

"Mother's worried Hitler will invade the Netherlands one day," Margot went on.

"What does Daddy think?" asked Anne.

"He thinks we're safe here."

"Good," said Anne. "Then I won't worry about it either. Besides," she added, "I don't have time for Hitler. I've got the summer vacation to think about. Months of swimming and sunbathing. I can't wait..."

This photograph, from Anne's photo album, shows Margot and Anne on a beach in Zandvoort, near Amsterdam, during their summer vacation.

Chapter 2
Broken glass

At the start of the new school year, Anne and Lies walked to school together as usual. Anne curled and twirled her hair around her fingers as she talked, casting smiles at the boy beside them.

"Anne Frank!" exclaimed Lies in a loud whisper. "You are such a flirt."

"No, I'm not," Anne giggled.

"Then stop looking at that boy."

"But he's looking at me!" Anne retorted. "Besides, I can't help it if he likes me."

"You just love people paying you attention," said Lies, laughing.

Anne felt she was having the best year ever. For her, 1937 was a golden time. She had a throng of friends, girls and boys, and there were family vacations to the lakes as well as trips to visit their cousins in Switzerland.

But as time passed, fear began to lurk at the back of Anne's mind, much as she tried to crush it. Aged nine, she overheard scraps of terrifying news from the grown-ups' conversations. They whispered about friends in Nazi Germany who had been rounded up and taken away to work in places called concentration camps. No one had heard from them since.

Words like *Kristallnacht* – "Night of broken glass" – rang in her head. Anne knew that on *Kristallnacht*, Jews in Germany had been beaten up and the windows of Jewish-owned shops and homes had been smashed in. The dark streets had glittered like a nightmare with shards of broken glass.

Safe in Amsterdam, the Franks tried to lead a normal life. But, the following year, 1939,

Edith was more worried than ever. "First Hitler invaded Poland, now Britain's declared war on Germany. It might be us next. What will happen then?"

This is a photograph of Boerneplatz synagogue in Frankfurt, the town of Anne's birth, burning on *Kristallnacht*. Nearly 1,000 synagogues were set on fire that night.

These are Jewish refugee children,
sent to England to escape the Nazis.

"Send the girls to us," wrote Otto's cousin
Milly, from England. "I know we're at war,
but if you think it's the least bit safe, please
send the children here."

But although Edith and Otto discussed it,
they decided to stay together as a family.
"We couldn't bear to part with the girls," Otto
wrote back. "They mean too much to us."

The following May, Anne and Margot had
their photographs taken as usual. Anne spent

a happy afternoon sticking the photos into her album. She studied them carefully. Now she was eleven, Anne took her appearance very seriously. She longed to look glamorous. Beside each one, she scribbled a note...

Oh, what a joke!

Whatever next?

Things are getting more serious, but there's still a smile left over for the funny parts.

This is a photograph of me as I wished I looked all the time. Then I might still have a chance of getting to Hollywood. But at present, I'm afraid I usually look quite different.

But, later that night, she couldn't sleep. The air was filled with a strange droning noise. She looked at her clock. It said four in the morning. The next moment there was a huge explosion, followed by another and then another. Anne raced into her parents' room.

"What's happening?" she cried.

Her parents were standing with Margot, staring out of their bedroom window. Anne went to look too. Massive planes were streaming across the sky. In the distance, fires burned and the smell of smoke seeped in through the open window.

Otto put his arm around Anne and held her close. "They're German planes, Anne," he said. "Hitler's invading."

18

Chapter 3

Invasion

Until daybreak, German and Dutch planes fought over Amsterdam's skies. That morning, the streets were filled with panic, as people tried to find out what was happening. Others stayed glued to their radios.

The next few days were punctuated with the piercing wail of air-raid sirens, warning everyone to take cover. The sirens were always followed by the sound of exploding bombs. Anne lay awake most

This photograph of bomb-damaged buildings was taken in Amsterdam in May 1940.

nights, shaking with fear. Then came the announcement on the radio: "Germans threaten to bomb the city of Rotterdam unless we surrender." Two hours before the deadline expired, the Germans bombed Rotterdam anyway. 900 people were killed. Fearing further bombings, the Netherlands surrendered – just four days after Hitler had invaded.

At first, life went on as normal. But, little by little, things did begin to change. It was announced that Jews had to register themselves, so the Nazis could find out exactly where they

This is a photograph of the formal entry of Nazi forces in Amsterdam. Dutch people have lined the streets to watch.

lived. Soon after, the Nazis began to pass anti-Jewish laws. Anne was furious. "We can't do anything," she grumbled to Lies and Sanne. "We have to walk everywhere. We're not allowed into parks or swimming pools..."

"I hate it," agreed Lies.

They had spent the morning flipping through fashion magazines and gossiping. Now they wanted to go out. But echoing down the street they heard the stomp! stomp! of marching footsteps. A group of Dutch Nazis were walking by, wearing their uniforms with pride.

The girls hid from view until the footsteps faded into silence. They'd heard stories of what Nazi soldiers did to Jews.

"Do you want to come up and see my outfit for Miep and Jan's wedding?" Anne suggested, to break the silence.

They raced inside. Anne proudly showed them her new coat and hat. "And," she added excitedly, "I'm going to have a new hairstyle for the occasion."

Anne felt that whenever she was with her friends, she had to stay cheerful. Margot,

Anne and Otto are on their way to Miep's wedding, on July 17, 1941. Anne is next to her father and is wearing her new coat and hat.

on the other hand, grew quieter than ever.

At the end of that summer, all the Jewish children from Anne's school were kept behind after assembly. The headmistress faced them from the front of the room. "I'm afraid you won't be allowed to return to this school next term," she began, her hands clasping and unclasping as she spoke. "The Nazis have passed a new law. Jewish children can no longer go to school with non-Jews."

Anne let out a cry and sobbed into her hands. She loved her school – why did she have to leave? She'd never see any of her non-Jewish friends now.

When Anne got home, Otto and Edith did their best to comfort her. "We'll send you and Margot to the Jewish Lyceum," Edith told her.

"It's so far away!" Anne cried.

"I know, I know," said Edith. "Please don't worry though. We must try to keep our lives as normal as possible."

But even loving parents were powerless to stop what was happening.

The following spring, the Nazis passed yet another law. All Jews had to sew a yellow star onto their clothes, with the word "Jood" on it, the Dutch for Jew.

"I'm scared to do anything now in case it's forbidden," said Anne's friend, Jacque. Anne knew just how she felt.

All Jews had to wear a star like this from April, 1942.

That year, the Franks celebrated the Jewish festival of Passover with the van Pels family. Otto and Mr. van Pels worked together, and suddenly it seemed as if the van Pelses were always at the Franks' house – the parents

This is a classroom photograph of Jewish school children. The children at the front can be seen wearing the "Jood" star.

talking together in hushed voices. Anne didn't take much notice. She was determined to have some fun still. She formed a ping-pong club with Jacque, Lies, Sanne and her friend Ilse, playing on the dining room table at Ilse's house.

Anne also had her birthday to look forward to. She was going to be thirteen.

"I already know what I'm getting," Anne told Lies. "I chose it myself! It's an autograph book, but I'm going to use it as a diary and write all my secrets in it!"

On the morning of Anne's birthday, Lies came by to walk to school with Anne. Peering into the Franks' sitting room to see Anne's presents, Lies noticed, not for the first time, how bare the room looked.

"The Franks must be selling off their furniture," Lies thought. "Perhaps they need the money."

That night, Anne wrote in her diary for the first time. "I hope I shall be able to confide in you completely, as I have never been able to do in anyone before, and I hope you will be a great source of comfort and support."

Otto was glad his daughter had a diary. He thought she would need it in the months to come.

"We may have to go into hiding," he said, as they strolled down the streets together. "Even though it will be hard for us to live cut off from the rest of the world."

"What do you mean?" Anne asked.

"You know how we've been sending our clothes and furniture to other people?" Otto began.

"I thought that was just to stop the Nazis from taking them?"

"Well, yes..." Otto replied. "But we don't want the Nazis to take us too. So we'll leave on our own, not wait for them to get us."

Anne looked scared. "But when, Daddy?"

"Don't worry. We'll take care of everything. Just enjoy your carefree life while you can."

Anne didn't reply. She was desperately hoping that day was still a long way off.

A week later, Anne was lying on the flat roof, lazily reading in the sun, when Margot rushed up to her.

"Father's received a call-up from the Nazis," she said, breathlessly. "Mother's gone to see Mr. van Pels."

Anne could feel her body start to shake. Everyone knew what a call-up was. It meant being sent to a concentration camp, and no one ever came back from those.

"He's not going," Margot declared. "Mother's gone to ask Mr. van Pels if we can go to our hiding place tomorrow. The van Pelses are going with us," she added.

This Jewish family is being sent to Westerbork, a transit camp in the Netherlands, after receiving their call-up notices. From Westerbork, most Jews were sent on to concentration camps in the east.

Anne and Margot sat in tense silence, waiting for their mother to return. Anne kept thinking of their father, visiting friends at the Jewish hospital, with no idea what was happening.

"I lied!" Margot burst out suddenly. "The call-up wasn't for Father. It was for me."

Anne was so shocked she started to cry.

"It's because I'm sixteen now. The Nazis are sending girls my age away."

"Daddy won't let you go," said Anne.

"No." Margot sank into her chair, then sprang up again. "We'd better start packing."

Anne found herself shoving the craziest things in her bag. Her diary, hair curlers, schoolbooks, some old letters. She couldn't concentrate. She was bursting with questions. "Where will we go?" she began. "Where will we hide?"

Margot began to explain what was going to happen. "Mr. Kleiman and Mr. Kugler, from Daddy's work, are going to help us. So are Miep and Jan, and Daddy's secretary, Bep."

Otto finally came back late that afternoon.

Miep arrived too and took with her bags full of clothes, promising to return later. The family sat together in silence. It was so hot, and everything felt very strange. Even though Anne knew it was her last night in her own bed, she fell straight to sleep. Early the next morning, she was gently shaken awake by her mother. "It's time to go, darling," she said.

This is the last photograph of the Frank family together, taken in 1941, the year before they went into hiding.

Outside, a warm rain had started to fall. The four Franks emerged from their house wearing as many of their clothes as possible. They couldn't take suitcases, or the Nazis would be onto them in a moment. Anne felt sure she was going to suffocate.

Margot rode ahead on her bicycle. At last, Anne's parents told her where they were going. "The hiding place is in Daddy's office building," Edith told her. "We were going to move next month, when everything would have been ready, but we have to go now because of Margot's call-up."

"In Daddy's office building?" Anne queried.

"Yes, there's a secret annex at the back of the building. No one would guess it, but there are lots of rooms there."

As soon as they arrived, Miep quickly led them through the office, down a long passage and up a wooden staircase. There, behind another door, lay the annex...

This is the front of Otto's office building, at 263 Prinsengracht, in Amsterdam. The Franks hid in the back part of the building, on the top two floors.

Chapter 4
The secret annex

Five months later, Anne was lying in bed, staring up at her bedroom wall. She had covered it with photographs of her family and her pictures of movie stars to make it seem more like home.

These are some of the photographs, and a postcard, that Anne pasted onto her bedroom wall. The photographs are of film stars, the Dutch royal family and Princesses Elizabeth and Margaret of England.

"It's amazing," Anne was thinking. "There are eight people all living in this tiny space."

A week after the Franks moved in, the van Pelses had come to join them. "Mr. van Pels tells terrible jokes and Mrs. van Pels is always scolding me," Anne grumbled to herself. "It's a shame their son, Peter, is so dull. But it's good to have other people around. If only I didn't have to share a room with the *exasperating* Mr. Pfeffer..."

As Anne turned, her bed made a loud creaking noise.

"Shh, shh," muttered Pfeffer, from his side of the narrow room.

Anne clenched her fists. "Next time he shushes me," she thought, "I'm going to shush him right back. But I know I mustn't moan... I *must* be reasonable."

Fritz Pfeffer had arrived in November, four months after the Franks. The van Pelses had immediately presented him with a *Guide to the Secret Annex*. Fritz needed to learn the rules of the annex quickly, so he didn't put everyone in hiding at risk.

```
x----------------------------------------x
         GUIDE TO THE SECRET ANNEX
   x----------------------------------------x


         A VAN PELS PRODUCTION*

           Open all year round
         Price: Free. Diet: Low-fat.
       Running water: In the bathroom
             (sorry, no baths).
   A tin tub may be used for washing after
     9:00am on Sundays. Residents may wash
       in the downstairs lavatory, kitchen,
         private office or front office,
             as they choose.
       Private radio: Available after 6:00pm.
         Rest hours: 10:00pm to 7:30am;
             10:15am on Sundays.
   To ensure the safety of all, rest hours
         must be strictly observed!
   Use of language: It is necessary to speak
     softly at all times. Only the language of
         civilized people may be spoken,
             thus no German.
   Lessons: A weekly correspondence course in
   shorthand (in Miep's name). Lessons in English,
   math and history for the children each day.
           Breakfast: 9:00am.
     Lunch: A light meal from 1:15pm to 1:45pm.
       Dinner: May or may not be a hot meal.
       Meal times depend on news broadcasts.
```

*Taken from Anne's diary

As soon as Pfeffer arrived, everyone pelted him with questions about the outside world.

"Things are getting worse for the Jews," he told them. "Night after night, the Nazis cruise the streets. They break into people's houses, looking for Jews in hiding. Anyone found is taken away to the camp at Westerbork."

There was silence after that. Miep had told them about Westerbork. The people there hardly got anything to eat. And the camps in Poland were even more terrible. The radio said Jews were being gassed there.

"Perhaps that's the quickest way to die," thought Anne. "It's so quiet here and we're safe, at least for now. I should be grateful. We're the lucky ones."

But it was hard to be grateful all the time. Being cooped up all day meant arguments broke out frequently, and Anne hated having to tiptoe around each day, keeping her voice to a whisper. "I long to be able to move around freely again," she confided to her diary. She was terrified, too, that they'd be discovered and shot.

As the war dragged on, things seemed to be getting worse. News reports on the radio told of battles being fought in Africa, Russia, Italy… "The whole world is at war," Anne wrote in her diary. "And the end is nowhere in sight."

When Anne peeked out from behind the curtains now, the children on the streets looked ragged and starving. As the months

A photograph of a Nazi raid on Dutch Jews. The Jewish men were rounded up and then sent to Mauthausen concentration camp in Austria.

passed, food became scarcer and scarcer. It was only the efforts of their helpers that kept the members of the annex alive.

Every day, Miep went out on her bicycle to find food for them all, often waiting for hours just to get a loaf of bread, while Bep smuggled in milk from the office supply. And every Saturday, Miep brought five books from the library.

"You have no idea how we long for Saturdays," Anne told Miep. "Books mean everything when you're cooped up. We couldn't do without your visits, either," she added. Anne knew that the office staff risked their lives to help them.

For the sake of their helpers, and for the others in hiding, Anne tried to stay cheerful and brave. But at times she felt as if her personality were splitting in two. When she was with the others she laughed and joked and chatted away. Only when she was alone, writing her diary, did she feel free to reveal her serious side. Sometimes she would flood her diary with her despair.

The atmosphere is stifling, sluggish, leaden, she wrote. "A deathly oppressive silence hangs over the house and clings to me as if it were going to drag me into the deepest regions of the underworld... I wander from room to room, climb up and down the stairs and feel like a songbird whose wings have been ripped off and who keeps hurling itself against the bars of its dark cage."

One night, Anne dreamed of Lies. She was dressed in rags, her face thin and worn. She looked at Anne with such sadness in her eyes. "Help me," she seemed to say, "rescue me from this hell!"

"But I can't help you!" Anne called out. "I can only stand by and watch while you and other Jews suffer and die." When Anne woke, she was crying. "What's happened to Lies?" she thought. "She's probably been taken away to the camps. Why have I been chosen to live, while she's probably going to die?"

For days after, Anne kept seeing those enormous eyes. They haunted her. She longed to talk to someone... "Daddy's the only one

This is the attic window in the secret annex – the only window that could be kept open for fresh air.

who understands me," she thought. "He's the most wonderful father in the world. But I can't talk to Mother. I feel so distant from her and Margot now."

After a while, she thought maybe she could talk to Peter. They began to spend more and more time together.

Peter was shy and withdrawn, but gradually,

Anne won his confidence. They would sit together by the window in the attic, looking out at the blue sky, the bare chestnut tree glistening with dew, the seagulls and other birds that glinted with silver as they swooped through the air. They looked in silence, Anne feeling entranced by a spell that shouldn't be broken with words.

Whenever Anne felt sad or frustrated, she and Peter would go up to the attic. "As long as you look fearlessly at the sky," Anne wrote in her diary, "you'll know that you're pure within and will find happiness once more." Anne's writing meant everything to her now. She poured out her thoughts and feelings into her diary and began to write stories of her own – short stories, fairy tales, the start of a novel...

Peter van Pels, in 1940, aged fourteen

"I'll tell you what," Anne announced over the kitchen table one morning, "being in hiding for two years is no picnic, especially in this war." Her voice sounded muffled – she was speaking through a handkerchief.

"What is that smell?" asked Margot.

"Lunch," replied Mrs. van Pels. "We're out of oil and as of tomorrow we won't have a scrap of butter. Today we're eating mashed potato and pickled kale."

"Urgh!" exclaimed Anne. "The thought of eating this muck makes me feel sick."

"Perhaps you should spend more time on your school work, like Margot," said Mrs. van Pels. "Then you'd have your studies to occupy your thoughts."

"She's just jealous because I'm so close to Peter," Anne thought. But deep down she knew she hadn't been bothering with her studies. Her thoughts had been filled with Peter, and there seemed no point in school work, with the end of the war so far away, like a fairy tale. That night, Anne thought about what she really wanted out of life... "To be a writer!" she realized.

Two months later, the members of the secret annex were crowded around the radio. "Today is D-Day!" announced the BBC.

"This is it!" cried Otto. "The invasion has begun! British and American troops have landed in France."

"Friends are on their way," said Anne.

"There's hope!" breathed Margot. "The war is coming to an end. Imagine, Anne, by October we could be back at school."

The summer passed in great excitement.

News reports came in thick and fast of invasion successes against the Germans. Sometimes, Anne felt overwhelmed by the chaos and suffering reported on the radio. But, when she looked up at the sky, she felt that somehow everything would change for the better, that peace would return once more. "In spite of everything," Anne wrote in her diary, "I still believe that people are good at heart."

This photograph shows a fleet of vessels, holding British, American and Canadian troops, landing in Nazi-occupied France on June 6, 1944. It is the beginning of the invasion of Western Europe.

The stairs leading from the office
to the secret annex

Chapter 5

Westerbork

August 4, 1944 was a warm, still summer's day. At the headquarters of the Nazi Secret Police, the telephone rang. An officer picked up the receiver and listened for a while. Then he quickly left the building accompanied by a number of Dutch police. They parked outside Otto's office and marched into the building. "We know everything," the Nazi officer announced. "You're hiding Jews and they're in this building. Take us to them."

Helplessly, Victor Kugler, the Franks' friend and helper, took the police up to the annex. The police went into each of the rooms, rounding everyone up, forcing them to put their hands in the air. Margot wept softly.

An hour later, they were out on the street, along with Kugler and Kleiman, being ordered into a police van.

"I'm sorry," Otto said to Kleiman, on their way to prison. "To think that you're sitting here among us, that we are to blame..."

"Don't give it another thought," Kleiman interrupted him. "I wouldn't have done it any differently."

Kleiman and Kugler were taken away for questioning. After three days in filthy overcrowded prisons, the eight members of the annex were sent on a train to Westerbork.

This photograph was taken in secret. It shows a group of Jews on their way to Westerbork with their luggage.

"At least we're still together," said Otto.

After the numbness of the past few days, Anne felt strangely cheerful. "Perhaps the war will end before they can send us to the death camps," she thought. "And right now, right this moment, I'm outside. I feel almost free. I can feel the sun on my face again."

At Westerbork, the Franks lined up to register. They were marked down as criminals for being in hiding, and sent to one of the punishment blocks. There, they were stripped of their clothes and handed blue overalls, marked with red thread to show they were criminals, and given wooden clogs to wear. Then the men had their heads shaved and the women had their hair shorn painfully short. Anne minded dreadfully about losing her hair.

Otto was sent to the men's barracks, Edith, Margot and Anne to the women's. "Don't worry," Edith told her daughters. "We'll still see Daddy in the evenings."

"Yes," whispered Anne, clinging to her mother as if she were a small child again.

Each day, work began at five in the morning, chopping up metal batteries. Anne was horrified when she realized what they had to do. "Chop open the batteries with a chisel and hammer," they were told. "Put tar in one basket and carbon bars in the other." It was messy work. The batteries gave off a kind of dust, and Margot and Anne couldn't stop coughing. "But at least we can talk!" Anne said to the girls, Janny and Lientje, sitting next to her. For lunch they received a piece of stale bread and a few spoonfuls of watery soup.

Margot eyed it dolefully. "I never thought we'd actually be caught," she said.

"I know," Anne replied. "But let's stay hopeful. The end of the war must come soon. If we can just stay here, we'll survive."

Otto helped calm his daughters too, visiting them at night to tell them stories.

A month later, a feeling of panic flooded through the camp. There was to be another transport out of Westerbork, to a camp in the east. A long train of cattle trucks rolled into Westerbork that night. By eleven the next morning, 1,019 people had been loaded on and the doors bolted shut. The van Pelses, Pfeffer and the Franks were among them.

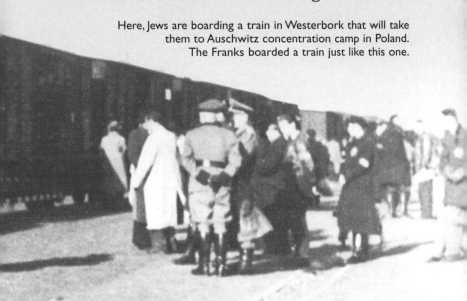

Here, Jews are boarding a train in Westerbork that will take them to Auschwitz concentration camp in Poland. The Franks boarded a train just like this one.

Chapter 6
The camps

The Franks stood pressed against the wall, clutching their bags. Cracks of light came in through grids of rusted wire netting. The journey went on and on. People jostled around, trying to get near the crack in the door, to get away from the stench. Anne was horribly tired and stiff. She wanted to lie down on the floor, but Otto wouldn't let her. "You'll be stepped on," he said. Anne saw that it was true. Every time someone tried to sit, feet trampled on them from all sides.

"Lean on me when you're tired," Otto said.

Every now and then, Anne was able to climb up and peer through the rusted wire netting. She caught glimpses of beautiful, endless cornfields. For a moment, she was able to forget she was on a train in the midst of a war.

Edith was busy with their overalls. She was trying to unpick the red thread, hoping that without it they could pretend they weren't convict prisoners.

No one knew which camp the train was going to. "Perhaps Auschwitz, in Poland," some whispered. It was a name that filled everyone with dread.

At the end of the third day, in the gathering dark, the train finally came to a stop.

The forbidding approach to Auschwitz-Birkenau by train

Rifle butts pounded on the door. "Jews out! Jews out!" shouted male voices.

Climbing out with stiff limbs, the first thing Anne saw was the glare of bright, bluish, neon lights. "Women to one side, men to the other," said a voice over a loudspeaker. With whips and cudgels, guards forced the men and women apart. Anne was shunted away from her father. Looking around, the last glimpse Otto had of his daughters were Margot's eyes, filled with terror.

This is a photograph of the selection process on the train platform at Auschwitz-Birkenau. All the people on the right have been selected as "fit" for work. Those on the far left are on their way to the gas chambers to die.

Next came another shout, "Get into rows of five."

A tall man with gleaming polished boots divided the women into two columns. One column was made up of the very old and the very young. Guards marched them away.

Everyone else, including Anne, her mother and sister were forced to walk in a different direction. On the way they passed buildings with huge clouds of black smoke pouring from the chimneys. And there was a smell. A horrible, horrible smell. "This is a death camp," Anne realized. "They kill people here."

"And that's where they burn the bodies," someone said behind her.

At the camp they were stripped, forced to shower and then shaved. Lastly, they were handed sack-like dresses and made to line up, so that each woman in turn could have a number tattooed on her arm.

Anne, Margot and Edith were sent to their barracks – block number 29. As Anne took in their new surroundings, she almost gagged. The stench of urine was everywhere.

Every morning, they woke at half past three to the sound of sharp whistles. Breakfast was a brown liquid slopped into their bowls.

Morning and night, in all weathers, they stood outside for their roll call, which could last for up to five hours. Margot and Anne always stood together, both very quiet and withdrawn. Then they marched half an hour to work, to dig an area of grass.

There was no point to the work, but the head prisoners, the kapos, ran among them screaming, "Faster! Faster!"

These women in Auschwitz have been classified as "able-bodied for work" and are being sent to the women's section of the camp known as BI.

For supper they had a slice of bread. It was Anne's job to distribute the bread among their block, which she always did fairly. At ten, they went into their barracks to try to sleep.

Edith's only thought now was for her daughters. She begged extra food for them when she could and kept them close to her.

Then the news came that another selection was to be made, this time to a factory where the work was less demanding. Anne was rejected as she had scabies, red sores on her body where lice had burrowed beneath her skin. Edith and Margot refused to go without her and Margot chose to go into the scabies barracks with Anne, to keep her company.

Edith was in despair without them. Each night, she went to the scabies barracks and dug a hole in the soft earth, so she could pass scraps of food to the children. By now, Margot had scabies too.

Days later, another selection was made. Edith, as an older woman, was kept behind at Auschwitz, but Margot and Anne were sent on.

The moment had come when Edith would be parted from her daughters. She had no idea if she would see them again. "The children! Oh God!" she screamed after them.

Anne and Margot were herded onto a train once more. No one knew where they were going and it was bitterly cramped and cold.

Four days later, they arrived at the Bergen-Belsen camp in Germany.

There, Anne and Margot were put to work in a shoe shed, unstitching shoes by hand. The work made Anne's hands bleed. Once again, they were existing only on a bowl of so-called soup and a slice of bread.

Anne grew thinner and thinner. She seemed to consist only of her eyes... eyes with a greenish glint. But the girls weren't broken yet.

Here, women prisoners at Bergen-Belsen are searching for scraps of food. By the time Margot and Anne arrived, the camp was heavily overcrowded with no proper accomodations and hardly any food.

At Bergen-Belsen they met up with Janny and Lientje, who they knew from Westerbork. Together, the Dutch girls celebrated Christmas, Hanukkah, New Year – all at once. They saved scraps of food, sang songs and told stories. Everyone tried their best not to cry, even though they were thinking about their loved ones.

A barbed wire fence ran through the middle of the camp. The conditions on the other side of the wire were meant to be slightly better. One day, Anne was told a girl she knew was in the other camp, and that she wanted to meet Anne at the wire fence.

Anne approached the wire – cold, hungry, shaven-headed – even though she knew the guards would shoot her just for going there. In the fading evening light, Anne could just make out Lies on the other side. She began to cry. "I don't have any parents any more," she sobbed.

Lies sobbed too. She told Anne her mother had died and that her father was sick in the camp hospital.

"We don't have anything to eat here," Anne went on. "And they've taken all our clothes."

"Meet me at eight tomorrow evening. I'll bring you food," Lies whispered.

The following night, Lies threw Anne a package over the fence, but Anne let out a cry.

"What's happened?" Lies called.

"Another woman caught it," Anne replied. "And she won't give it back."

The next evening, Lies threw Anne another bundle full of food. This time, Anne caught it. But that was the last time Lies and Anne saw each other.

Margot had fallen ill with dysentry and was sent to the sick bay. Anne went with her. "Don't go there," Lientje told her, "you'll die."

But it was warm in the sick bay and there were only two of them in one bunk. "We are together and we have our peace," Anne said.

Margot hardly said anything. She had a fever and her mind was wandering, but she smiled weakly.

That March, another disease spread through Bergen-Belsen – this time it was typhus. Anne and Margot both caught it. They lay in the bunk by the barrack door, where the cold wind came stinging in. Other inmates heard their cries, "Close the door! Close the door!"

Lientje and Janny came to visit them. Margot had fallen from her bunk the night before and was only half-conscious. Anne was feverish but loving. "Margot will sleep well and when she sleeps I don't need to get up anymore."

Margot was too weak to survive the fall and the shock killed her. After that, Anne gave in to her illness. She died sometime in March, thinking her mother and father were dead, believing herself alone in the world.

A month after Anne died, Bergen-Belsen was liberated by British troops. In this photograph, the liberators are watching the typhus-infested barracks being burned. A poster of Hitler hangs on the barrack wall, soon to go up in flames.

ANNE FRANK'S DIARY

Of the eight members of the annex, Anne's father Otto was the only one to survive. After the war was over, he returned to Amsterdam to look for his daughters, desperately hoping they were still alive. There he met Janny, who had to tell him that both Margot and Anne were dead.

Once Miep knew Anne wasn't coming back, she told Otto she'd saved Anne's diary. She gave it to him saying, "Here is your daughter's legacy to you."

There's a line in the diary that reads, "I want to go on living after I'm dead..." It was that line that made Otto finally decide to publish the diary as a book. Since its first publication in 1947, Anne's diary has been translated into 50 languages and sold over 25 million copies. Anne Frank still lives on.

"A person who's happy will make others happy; a person who has courage and faith will never die in misery!"

Anne Frank's diary,
March 7, 1944

Otto devoted the rest of his life to Anne's diary, making it his mission, "to bring Anne's message to as many people as possible."

In 1953, Otto married Fritzi Geiringer, and became stepfather to her daughter, Eva. Fritzi, like Otto, was a concentration camp survivor, whose husband and son had died at Auschwitz. Fritzi helped Otto with his work, spending several hours each day replying to letters from readers of Anne's diary.

Ever since the diary was first published, people had knocked on the door of 263 Prinsengracht, asking to be shown the secret annex. In 1960, it was finally opened as a museum, called The Anne Frank House. Over 800,000 people now visit the museum every year. Many countries have memorials to Anne Frank and June 12, Anne's birthday, has become Anne Frank Day.

All over the world, Anne is remembered for her writing, her courage, her hopes for the future and her faith in people. She has also become a symbol – for the pointlessness and suffering of war.

TIMELINE

1926 – (November 16) Margot Frank is born in Frankfurt, Germany.

1929 – (June 12) Anne Frank is born in Frankfurt, Germany.

1933 – Hitler is granted the powers of a dictator for four years in Germany.
(June) Otto Frank moves to Amsterdam.
(December) Edith & Margot join Otto in Amsterdam.

1934 – Anne joins her family in Amsterdam & goes to Montessori school.

1935 – Anti-Jewish laws are passed in Germany.

1938 – (November 9-10) *Kristallnacht* "Night of Broken Glass"

1939 – Germany conquers Poland. Britain & France declare war on Germany.

1940 – Otto Frank's business moves to 263 Prinsengracht.
(May 10) Germany invades the Netherlands.
(May 14) Dutch forces surrender.

1941 – (September) Margot & Anne Frank are transferred to Jewish school.

1942 – (June 12) Anne receives a diary as a birthday present.
(July 6) The Frank family goes into hiding.
(July 13) The van Pels family joins the Frank family in the annex.
(November 17) Fritz Pfeffer moves into the annex.

1944 – (June 6) D-Day: British, American & Canadian troops invade Normandy.
(August 4) The people hiding in the annex are arrested.
(August 8) They are transported to Westerbork and on
(September 3) are sent to Auschwitz-Birkenau.
(October) Margot & Anne are transferred to Bergen-Belsen.

1945 – (January) Edith Frank dies in Auschwitz.
(January 27) Auschwitz-Birkenau is liberated by the Russian army.
(March) Anne & Margot die.
(April 15) Bergen-Belsen is liberated by British troops.
(May 5) Liberation of the Netherlands
(May 8) VE (Victory in Europe) Day marks the end of the war
in Europe.
(June 3) Otto Frank returns to Amsterdam.

1947 – Anne's diary is published as The Annex (*Het Achterhuis*) in Dutch.

1951 – Anne's diary is published in English.

1960 – 263 Prinsengracht is opened as a museum, known as The Anne
Frank House.